BUILDING A

STADIUM

BY ANGIE SMIBERT

AMICUS | AMICUS INK

Sequence is published by Amicus and Amicus Ink
P.O. Box 1329, Mankato, MN 56002
www.amicuspublishing.us

Library of Congress Cataloging-in-Publication Data
Names: Smibert, Angie, author.
Title: Building a stadium / by Angie Smibert.
Description: Mankato, Minnesota : Amicus, [2019] | Series: Sequence. Amazing structures |
  Audience: Grade 4 to 6. | Includes bibliographical references and index.
Identifiers: LCCN 2017044773 (print) | LCCN 2017056947 (ebook) | ISBN 9781681515144
  (pdf) | ISBN 9781681514321 (library binding) | ISBN 9781681523521 (pbk.)
Subjects: LCSH: Stadiums--Design and construction--Juvenile literature.
Classification: LCC TH4714 (ebook) | LCC TH4714 .S65 2019 (print) | DDC 690/.5827--dc23
  LC record available at https://lccn.loc.gov/2017044773

Editor: Wendy Dieker
Designer: Veronica Scott and Ciara Beitlich
Photo Researcher: Holly Young

Photo Credits: Grafissimo/iStock cover; Filipe Frazao/Shutterstock 5; Andrew Holt/Alamy 6; Rawpixel.com/Shutterstock 9; by Danilo_Vuletic/Shutterstock 10; Roman Kadarjan/Alamy 13; August Schwerdfeger/WikiCommons 14–15; James Boardman/Alamy 17; Joe Ferrer/Alamy 18; Jeff Bukowski/Shutterstock 21; Tom Szczerbowski/Getty 22–23; haylocka/iStock 25; Theodore Silvius/Alamy 26; Andy Clayton–King/AP 29

Printed in China

HC 10 9 8 7 6 5 4 3 2 1
PB 10 9 8 7 6 5 4 3 2 1

We Need a Stadium!

News flash! A professional football team is moving to the city. But there's nowhere for the team to play. A stadium must be built. It has to be big enough to seat up to 70,000 fans. But for a project that big, the city wants a stadium for other sports and big concerts. They get to work on a stadium everyone can use.

A stadium is designed so thousands of people can see the action from any seat.

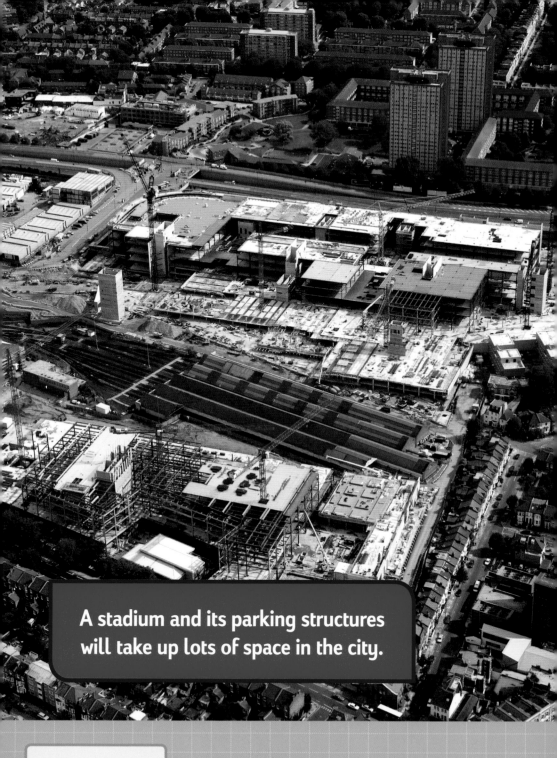

A stadium and its parking structures will take up lots of space in the city.

Choose a building site.

. . . L O A D I N G . . . L O A D I N G

Planning and Designing

Planning starts with choosing a site to build on. The football team owner and the city agree to split the construction costs. They pick a site downtown for the new stadium. This place is close to buses and the subway. The site also has room for lots of parking.

Next, building companies submit **bids**. Bids are documents that tell how much the stadium will cost. A bid also tells how long it should take to build. The city picks the company with the best bid. The winning company gets to work. They hire a team to lead the building project.

Choose a building site.

YEAR 1 ⟶

ADING . . . LOADING

Collect bids;
select a design team.

The building company puts together information about how they will do the building project.

JANUARY
FEBRUARY
MARCH
APRIL
MAY

25%
65%
75%

LSM/VK	EJ+EO	IDGH	EJ+EO	IDGH	EJ+EO	IDGH	EJ+EO
▲ 24.7050	▲ 86.560	0.650	86.560	▲ 0.650	57.030	▲ 0.650	57.030
47.0540	▲ 57.030	807.5	57.030		5.7540		5.7540
▲ 6760.70	▲ 5.7540	0.607	5.7540	▲ 807.5	0.7540	▲ 807.5	0.7540
▲ 34.7080	▲ 0.7540	540.5	0.7540	▲ 540.5	86.560	▲ 540.5	86.560

ADING...LOADING...LOADING...

9

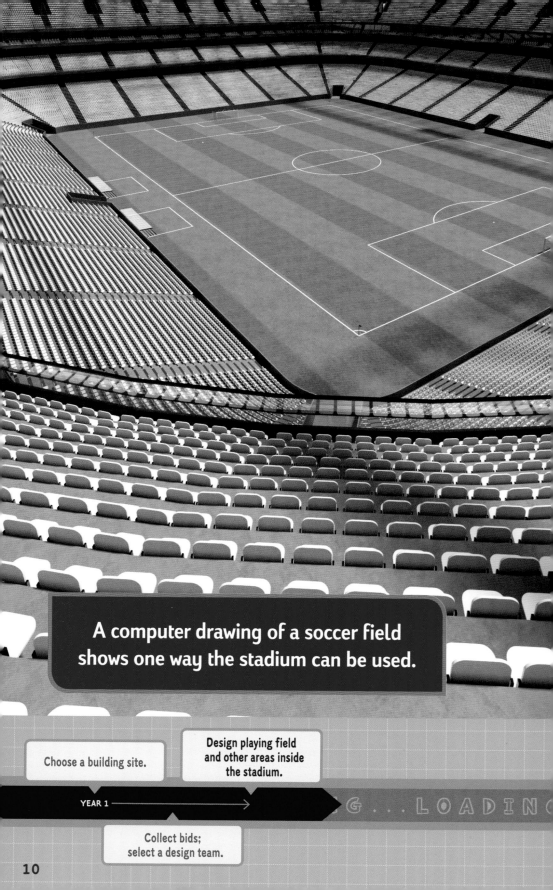

A computer drawing of a soccer field shows one way the stadium can be used.

Choose a building site.

Design playing field and other areas inside the stadium.

YEAR 1

G . . . L O A D I N

Collect bids; select a design team.

The company hires a team of **engineers** and **architects**. They design the stadium so that people can see the action from any seat. They also work to make sure the playing field can be changed for different events. Fans can watch football, soccer, or even a concert. **Interior designers** on the team plan offices, shops, and restaurants.

Putting It All Together

Construction crews first need to prepare the site. They tear down some old buildings. Then graders level out the ground. This gives the builders a flat surface to build on. Crews also dig out the area for the playing field. Then they put down layers of sand and gravel. This will be a good base for the **turf**.

Choose a building site.

Design playing field and other areas inside the stadium.

YEAR 1

LOADING

Collect bids; select a design team.

Tear down buildings; prepare playing field site.

A bulldozer pushes dirt around the construction site.

Tall tower cranes are set up while another crew works on the foundation.

Choose a building site.

Design playing field and other areas inside the stadium.

Build foundation.

YEAR 1 ⟶ YEAR 2

Collect bids; select a design team.

Tear down buildings; prepare playing field site.

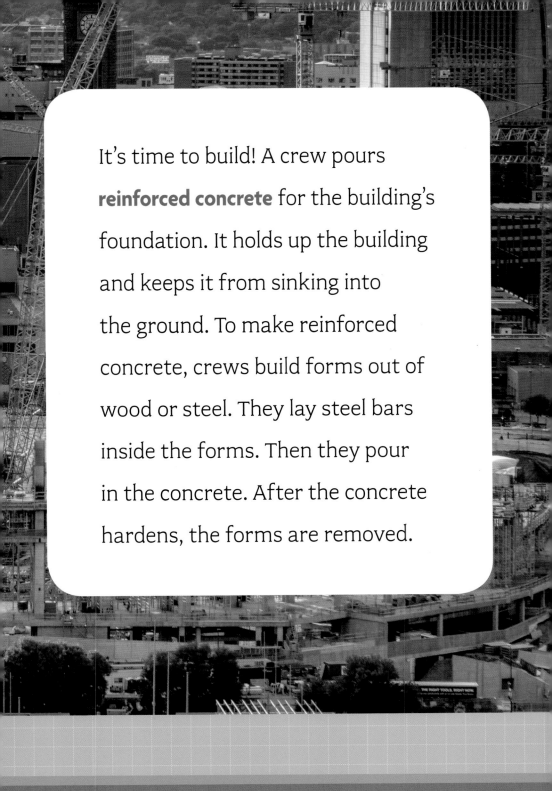

It's time to build! A crew pours **reinforced concrete** for the building's foundation. It holds up the building and keeps it from sinking into the ground. To make reinforced concrete, crews build forms out of wood or steel. They lay steel bars inside the forms. Then they pour in the concrete. After the concrete hardens, the forms are removed.

Next, crews build the stands. Cranes lift large concrete sections called risers into place. The seats will be placed on the risers. In a stadium, each row of seats is higher than the one below it. That way everyone can see the action. The risers are made up of concrete sections. These sections are cast at a factory and shipped to the construction site.

Choose a building site.

Design playing field and other areas inside the stadium.

Build foundation.

YEAR 1

YEAR 2

Collect bids; select a design team.

Tear down buildings; prepare playing field site.

Ship risers to stadium site; install risers.

Before the seats are put in, the concrete risers look like a set of stairs.

Choose a building site.

Design playing field and other areas inside the stadium.

Build foundation.

YEAR 1 ———————————————→ YEAR 2 ————————

Collect bids; select a design team.

Tear down buildings; prepare playing field site.

Ship risers to stadium site; install risers.

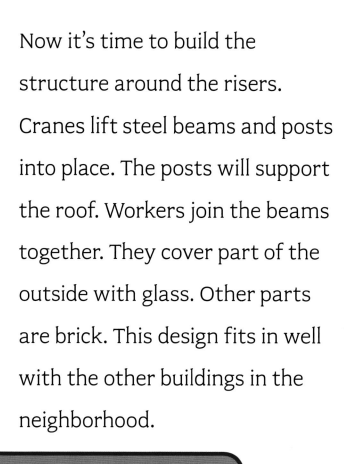

Now it's time to build the structure around the risers. Cranes lift steel beams and posts into place. The posts will support the roof. Workers join the beams together. They cover part of the outside with glass. Other parts are brick. This design fits in well with the other buildings in the neighborhood.

Tall cranes lift beams to make the building structure.

Lift beams into place; build walls.

The roof is next. This city has cold, snowy winters, so the stadium will have a permanent roof. Many stadiums have no roof at all—or a **retractable roof**. This stadium's roof will be covered with a clear, very strong plastic-like material. The fans and players will feel like they're outside. But they won't have to deal with the weather.

This stadium roof will protect fans and players from weather, but still lets in light.

Choose a building site.

Design playing field and other areas inside the stadium.

Build foundation.

YEAR 1 ————————————————————→ YEAR 2

Collect bids; select a design team.

Tear down buildings; prepare playing field site.

Ship risers to stadium site; install risers.

Attach roof.

YEAR 3

DING... LOADING...

Lift beams into place;
build walls.

Natural grass is laid for a soccer match in the stadium.

Choose a building site.

Design playing field and other areas inside the stadium.

Build foundation.

YEAR 1 ——————————————————→ YEAR 2 ——————

Collect bids; select a design team.

Tear down buildings; prepare playing field site.

Ship risers to stadium site; install risers.

Back inside, crews put the turf on the field. It's a thick fabric that looks like grass. The turf comes in large rolls. Crews unfurl each one. Then they glue and sew the edges of the fabric together. For concerts, workers can cover the field with special flooring. Crews install large high-definition screens on each end of the field.

Attach roof.

→ YEAR 3 →

Lift beams into place; build walls.

Install turf; install giant TV screens.

Crews install the seats and press boxes in the stands. Locker rooms and offices are also built. Crews work on the restaurants and shops. The interior is decorated to match the football team's colors. Electricians install TV screens and wi-fi connections throughout the **concourse**. Fans won't miss any of the action.

Some seats in the stadium are big and comfortable.

Choose a building site.

Design playing field and other areas inside the stadium.

Build foundation.

YEAR 1 ——————————————————————————————→ YEAR 2

Collect bids; select a design team.

Tear down buildings; prepare playing field site.

Ship risers to stadium site; install risers.

Attach roof.

Install seating;
finish all interior spaces.

→ YEAR 3

ADING...

Lift beams into place;
build walls.

Install turf;
install giant TV screens.

Choose a building site.

Design playing field and other areas inside the stadium.

Build foundation.

YEAR 1 ⟶ YEAR 2

Collect bids; select a design team.

Tear down buildings; prepare playing field site.

Ship risers to stadium site; install risers.

Lastly, construction crews pave the parking lots. They also plant grass, flowers, and trees around the stadium. Electricians install lighting and electric signs outside. Painters finish painting the outside of the building. Window cleaners clean the giant glass walls. After four years, the stadium is finished.

The finished stadium is ready for the city's big events.

Attach roof.

Install seating; finish all interior spaces.

→ YEAR 3 →

Lift beams into place; build walls.

Install turf; install giant TV screens.

Pave parking areas; plant grass, flowers, and trees; install lights and signs.

Kickoff Time!

A large crowd gathers outside the stadium. The owner of the football team cuts the ribbon. The new stadium is open! The public gets a tour of the new stadium and meets the players. On Sunday, the football team takes the field in the first game of the season. The fans love how open the stadium feels. And everyone can see the action!

Choose a building site.

Design playing field and other areas inside the stadium.

Build foundation.

YEAR 1 ─────────────────────────────────────▶ YEAR 2 ──────

Collect bids; select a design team.

Tear down buildings; prepare playing field site.

Ship risers to stadium site; install risers.

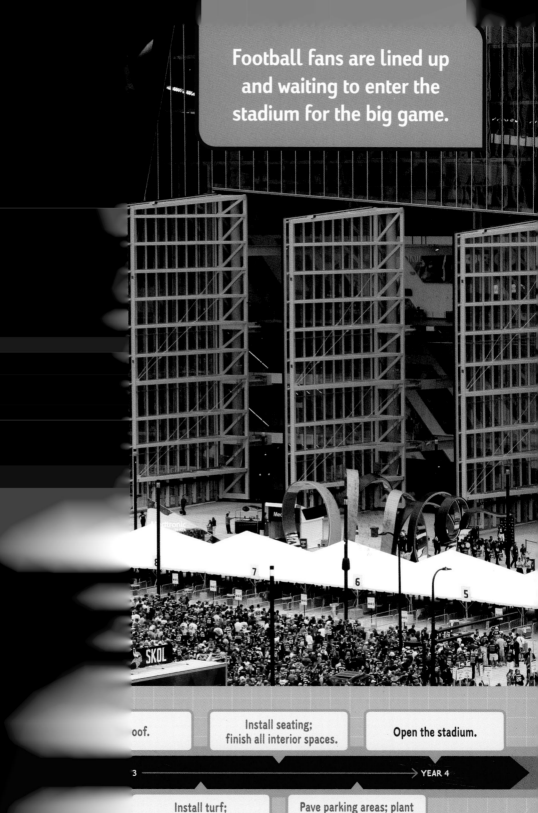

Football fans are lined up and waiting to enter the stadium for the big game.

oof.

Install seating; finish all interior spaces.

Open the stadium.

3 ────────────────────────→ YEAR 4

Install turf; install giant TV screens.

Pave parking areas; plant grass, flowers, and trees; install lights and signs.

GLOSSARY

architect A person who designs buildings.

bid A document building companies put together outlining how they will get a project done; it includes project cost and timeline.

concourse The hallways and gathering places around an event space or playing field.

engineer A person who studies the best way a structure can be designed and built for a particular place.

foundation The base of a building that supports the structure.

interior designer A person who specializes in designing, decorating, and furnishing interiors of buildings.

reinforced concrete Concrete that is poured over a grid of steel bars in order to strengthen the concrete; concrete is a building material made from a mixture of broken stone or gravel, sand, cement, and water that hardens upon drying.

retractable roof A roof that can be moved away to leave an open top.

turf A grass or grass-like surface that covers a playing field.

READ MORE

Lowell, Barbara. *Engineering AT&T Stadium.* Minneapolis: Abdo Publishing, 2017.

Mullins, Matt. *How Did They Build That Stadium?* Ann Arbor, Mich.: Cherry Lake, 2010.

Rowell, Rebecca. *Building Stadiums.* Minneapolis: Focus Readers, 2017.

WEBSITES

Lego Stadiums - Brick Model Designs
http://www.brickmodeldesign.com/stadiums/

PBS Building Big
www.pbs.org/wgbh/buildingbig/

Vikings US Bank Stadium Construction Time-Lapse | NFL
https://youtu.be/qB1S6CvvwUU

INDEX

ABOUT THE AUTHOR

Angie Smibert is the author of several young adult and middle grade novels, including the Memento Nora series, many short stories, and numerous educational titles just like this one. She was also a science writer at NASA's Kennedy Space Center for many, many years. Once upon a time, she even worked at an architecture and engineering firm that built amazing structures.